PRAISE FOR *WHITE MOON IN A POWDER BLUE SKY*

"Enchanting, extraordinary, and evolutionary—from the 'physics for poets' movement of 30 years ago, Dargis leads us into a much needed 'poetics for physicists' movement today."

—Thomas Brophy, PhD Physics, Executive Dean, California Institute for Human Science, *The Mechanism Demands a Mysticism: An Exploration of Spirit, Matter and Physics*

"I had a sense of peace while reading this book, which is a substantial contribution to how it is possible to bring together quantum theory, consciousness, and a connection to one's higher self."

—Patricia S. Maloof, PhD Medical Anthropology, *Body-Mind-Spirit: Toward a Biopsychosocial-Spiritual Model of Health*, an online publication of the National Center for Cultural Competence, Georgetown University

"Brilliant, thought-provoking, and therapeutic read! This book spoke to my soul."

—Lynn Jaffee, *Simple Steps: The Chinese Way to Better Health*

"Julie shares her journey with authenticity not often heard in today's world."

—Flossie Park, Sound Healer, Metaphysical Teacher, Director of Yoga Teacher Training at The Soul of Yoga

"Julie teaches that we are spirit, mind, and body—trauma drives them apart, and intuitive guidance is the pathway to a harmonious life."

—Brigit Viksnins, MAT, RCST®, SEP, Alchemical by Alignment, Bodywork for Trauma Resolution and Embodiment of Spirit

WHITE MOON IN A
POWDER BLUE SKY

9.19.16
To Leslie —
with love
Julie

Also by Julie R. Dargis

Seven Sonnets
Pit Stop in the Paris of Africa
Reader's Guide: Pit Stop in the Paris of Africa

White Moon in a Powder Blue Sky

A Primer in Healing from Both Sides of the Veil in Memoir, Sonnets, and Prose

JULIE R. DARGIS

INDIE HOUSE PRESS

Copyright © 2016 by Julie R. Dargis
All rights reserved.

No part of this publication may be used in any manner whatsoever without the prior written permission of the author, except for the inclusion of brief quotations contained in critical articles or reviews. For inquires, contact the author at www.IndieHousePress.org.

ISBN: 0692691979
ISBN-13: 978-0692691977

Printed in the United States of America

Library of Congress Control Number: 2016908171
Indie House Press, Carlsbad, CA

Design by Ryan Scheife, Mayfly Design, Minneapolis, MN

For Rosa Felicetta,
Grams, and A. T.
with love

CONTENTS

Acknowledgments xi
Preface xiii
Introduction xix

Part One: Evolution Revolution

At the Root of the World 3

The Realm of Duality 4

Two Corps, One Mission 5

Tolerance, Freedom, and Peace 6

The Land of Eternity 7

Ode to MSF @ Kunduz 9

Bound by My Footsteps 10

Part Two: The Relativity of Choice

Surrender to Gaia 15

Fun with Physics 16

Radio Flyer 17

Falling to Grace 18

The Sound of Silence 19

If Midnight Were Noon 20

Free Will to Choose 21

    Plasma Power 22

    Double-Blind Were We 23

    The Great Halls of Science 25

    The Shadow of Power 26

Part Three: Both Sides of the Veil

    The Cloak of Consciousness 29

    Fight or Flight 30

    White Light 31

    Bach Flower Power 32

    The Current of the Streetcars 33

    The Veil of Forgiveness 34

    The Writing on the Window 36

    When Spirit Calls 37

    The Climb to Assisi 38

    Future Perfect 39

    Spirit Animal 40

    The Echo of a Whisper 41

    Ask and It Is Given 42

    White Moon in a Powder Blue Sky 43

Postscript 45

Author's Note 49

Notes 53

About the Author 55

ACKNOWLEDGMENTS

To Catherine Bachy, Pam Bohlken, Mackenzie Hanson, Susan Vorderbruggen, and Sarah Wilson, thank you for being my beta readers. Your many insights and suggestions have enhanced this book with pure and positive energy. To Phyllis Theroux, who taught me how to neatly hang my paragraphs in a row and then to arrange them in a vase, your words kept nudging me back to where I needed to be. To Victoria Danzig, thank you for your magical insights into the field and for immediately—and intuitively—knowing. Many thanks also to Federico Emmanuel Miraglia, for your clarifications from the quantum world of particle physics (included as notes herein). Thank you to my loved ones, past and present. And to spirit, my incredible teachers and guides, thank you for the netting, tightly knotted in all directions in time with your undying respect for my free will.

PREFACE

Through an exploration of energy healing as it relates to quantum theory, consciousness, and the connection to one's higher self, we can begin to appreciate the mysteries of what Einstein termed "spooky action at a distance." This action, which is merely energy, is nothing to fear. By considering how we continue to be connected to our loved ones and spirit through an eternal, unending field of energy, we gain a deeper appreciation for what our lives are truly meant to be.

This book explores the nature of reality that revolves alongside the magical world of spirit. By giving equal play to the physical and subtle worlds, more than what is currently observable through the eyes of science comes into focus. Complementary modes of energy healing such as Traditional Chinese Medicine, Ayurveda, Homeopathy, Pranic Healing, and Reiki, among others, are demystified.

Although *spirit*, as defined in most dictionaries, is a singular pronoun, in this book I use it as a collective noun. The word comes from the Latin word *spiritus*, meaning "breath." To understand where spirit resides, one needs to consider the definition of consciousness. My personal "ontological" definition of consciousness includes the soul (our timeless spirits or higher selves) as part of the greater consciousness. Although we incarnate as individual personalities in each lifetime, our higher selves retain all of our life lessons and remain "tethered" to the eternal, collective consciousness through the subtle, causal body. Within this greater consciousness, the collective of individual spirits dissolves into "oneness."

On the other side of the veil, our loved ones and spirit live on with no constraints in either space or time. We know this from the many accounts of those who have had and documented near-death experiences (NDEs). For those who have had NDEs and have chosen to come back and continue their soul work in the three-dimensional[1] plane of Earth, they do so with a renewed commitment to teach others about love.

In my first book, *Pit Stop in the Paris of Africa* (2013), what I thought was going to be a travelogue of living and working overseas turned out to be so much more. With each chapter, I continued to unleash a profound sense of healing. But it was only in the last pages that I mentioned the word *love*. And yet my current belief is that there are only two choices on the road to healing: fear or love.

When I returned home to the United States from Rwanda after the genocide, love was the furthest thing from my mind. Instead, I was embroiled in exhaustion and sadness. I began working with a therapist who had previously worked with Vietnam veterans. Time and again, after I returned from my more difficult postings overseas, he helped me to work through my trauma.

Over the years, I have lived and worked in some of the most austere political environments around the world, in places like Chad, Rwanda, Somalia, and South Sudan. I was in Serbia prior to and during the bombing and in Afghanistan and Pakistan during ongoing and protracted conflict. I was a humanitarian aid worker, supporting refugees on the front lines, assisting with reconstruction efforts after natural disasters, and working with communities as they rebuilt their lives in the absence of peace. Coping mechanisms, created through childhood and past life traumas, were my badges of honor. But the more I steeled myself against conflict, the more I shielded myself against love.

My life once revolved around war, conflict, and natural disasters, but I have traded in that life for a quieter one of study and reflection. Life for me now centers on the study of the mind-body-spirit connection. Poetry was once a vehicle for me to find solace in the chaotic world around me. I am now applying it to *thought experiments* to better understand the subject matter of quantum theory, consciousness, and subtle energy.

Thought experiments are defined as experiments that are conducted in the imagination. Philosophers and scientists use them to consider a hypothesis or test theories when a physical experiment is not possible to conduct.

As a poet, I use them to frame a concept within the creative constraints of the sonnet structure, to see what will emerge in terms of understanding as I think through an aspect or paradox of quantum theory.

Ultimately, we all view the world from our own unique perspectives. Some believe that the world around us is processed solely within the gray matter of our brains. Others tell us that what we experience happens in a variety of electromagnetic fields outside of ourselves, within layers of multidimensional, subtle bodies. Still others tell us that the world we live in is merely an illusion. I say: *To each our own*. Each perspective has its merits, and most allow for spirited debate.

When I began my studies in integral health at the California Institute for Human Science, one of my first classes was Cosmology and the Nature of Reality, a graduate seminar with three physicists and myself. Unlike my classmates, I had no prior training in physics, although I have had a lifelong interest in quantum physics, reading widely over the years on a variety of quantum theories, including chaos and complexity theories. I also had read about the application of quantum physics as it related to the power of thought and the placebo effect. Nonetheless, each week in class I was utterly lost as I tried to "keep up" with my classmates.

One morning, after waking up in a panic, wondering how I was going to complete the class, I had an epiphany.

The message I received was that I was not a scientist, and no matter how hard I tried, I was never going to understand the physics and mathematics of this course through the lens of a scientist. Being a poet, I needed to use what came most naturally to me to understand "the matter at hand" in my own way. When I began writing sonnets to sort through the subject matter, I was able to relax, and this is when I started to learn.

I hope that the contents of this book resonate with readers and encourage them to explore the world of energy healing for themselves. By doing so, one is simply exploring how they can add alternative and complementary modalities to their current wellness repertoires to further achieve and sustain a state of well-being.

I also hope that readers will consider how they, too, can use their own unique voices in fresh and inspired ways. By expressing ourselves openly, without fear, we create inner pathways to healing. This healing arrives in the form of waves, and these waves flow outward. We affect those around us. Once our own personal ripple of peace begins to flow, it saturates our homes and flows out into our communities. By choosing a path that leads to self-healing, together we build a world of peace.

INTRODUCTION

*I*n this collection of poetry and prose, I cross the divide from an outer world of conflict to an inner world of peace. The result is a volume of work documenting this transformation in three interrelated pathways. As such, I have laid out the structure of this book in a three-card spread as if it were an oracle card reading.

Oracle cards have been used for centuries as divination tools. Many readers may be familiar with tarot cards. The cards I prefer to use are more aligned with the angelic realm, and the readings that I do are meant to connect clients with their higher selves. My role is merely one of facilitator in the process of self-directed healing.

Some of the oracle card decks that I use in readings have different meanings for the upright and reversed positions of the individual cards. Yet, drawing a card in the reversed position does not result in a negative message. Rather, it is an opportunity for one to consider a question or a situation from a different perspective. A shift in perspective is often the first step on the pathway to healing.

When I do oracle card readings for clients, I often begin with the three-card spread. In this spread, three cards are selected and laid out side-by-side in a row. Before we begin, I inform the client that the cards represent the immediate past, the present, and the immediate future.

Most often, the insights from each card coincide, relative to its position, to the client's current lifeline. But just as easily, a card in the past position may resonate with the clients' future; or the card in the future position may be more aligned with his or her immediate past, as there is no space or time outside of our universe.

"Part One: Evolution Revolution" reconsiders war and conflict-related trauma resulting from my humanitarian work overseas. Inherent in the writing presented in this section is the power of forgiveness.

"Part Two: The Relativity of Choice" explores the world of quantum physics and consciousness within the limitless possibilities of the present moment. True to the approach taken by physicists and other scientists around the world, this work initially draws on intuition and includes thought experiments in poetry and prose.

"Part Three: Both Sides of the Veil" ventures into intuitive communication with spirit and the subsequent healing that can result with support from the spirit world, linking past and present with the future.

As is often the case with oracle card readings, the deepest insights tend to come into focus days or even months after the cards have been pulled. For this reason, I have also included two additional sections.

In "Postscript," I illustrate how spirit tends to turn up the volume if we neglect to listen or heed their signs. This section also includes ways in which spirit communicates with us. In the "Author's Note," I share a personal experience in meditation that brought forth a parting, universal message.

Finally, on the website for the book, readers who wish to explore some of the concepts presented in this book more deeply for themselves can find information on courses, teachers, and a reading list on the mind-body-spirit connection.

—Julie R. Dargis
Carlsbad, CA
July 14, 2016

Part One

Evolution Revolution

At the Root of the World

We did not come here to save the world. We came here to save ourselves. In doing so, we will return the earth to its natural state of being. To be more in tune with nature, we can begin by tapping more intently into ourselves. By connecting to our higher hearts, we become more aligned with our higher selves. That which we seek also resides in nature. At the root of the world lies the promise of peace. Within its grasp, nature holds the essence to heal. Never one to discriminate, gravity unites us all.

The Realm of Duality

Love vs. Fear
Belief vs. Doubt
Light vs. Darkness

As the swat team advanced, I thrust myself
Against the wall, away from the windows.
Bound by fear for a moment in time, my
Hands held high, I was one with the others.
When we were freed, I stood frozen, my hands
Still up in the air. "You can put them down
Now, ma'am," the officer said. Slowly, I
Complied. Shuffling out with the rest, I crossed
The roundabout, back to my daily life.
At the stone fountain… *"to be frightened by*
Daylight because one can see, and darkness
Because one cannot…"[2] spilled from the waters.
As they flowed through centuries, the words of
Victor Hugo filled the basin below.

Two Corps, One Mission

The marine corps calls it "Stab Ops." In my
Corps—the Peace Corps—one need only turn a
Phrase to understand the other side of
Peace and stability operations.
Crossing cultures two hundred thousand strong,
Speaking the world's languages, more than white
Robes and sandals cover our hearts, carry
Our feet. Some of us walk on torn tire treads.
Along the same road, Americans all—
Both carry the flag of freedom. Down with
Tyranny! Never again! Accords of
Peace. *Kumbaya* an echo of *Ooh rah!*
Two rights. Neither wrong. Each called to duty
Led by honor. Two corps. One mission. Peace.

Tolerance, Freedom, and Peace

Pitch with us tolerance, freedom, and peace
In churches, synagogues, temples, and mosques.
Stand up with our friends at home and abroad.
Let respect choose the words we use wisely.
In Morocco, Mali, throughout Asia,
Eastern Europe, across the Middle East,
Peace Corps volunteers are welcome in homes.
We live together as one in global
Communities. Humanitarians
Working in Turkey, Greece, and Syria
Attest to the same. Islamophobic
Rhetoric, spinning in news cycles, is
Staining our communities with chatter.
Can you not hear all our cries to stand down?

The Land of Eternity

"Perhaps this is a good time to clarify the difference between connecting with your higher self and your ego. You are on to something, exploring the discernment between your higher self, which you are only now beginning to glimpse, and your ego, which tends to interrupt.

"When connecting to your intuition, you learned to differentiate your intuition from emotion. Now you must learn to differentiate me from your ego. One way is through pronouns. When I am speaking to you, I talk to *you*. Your ego uses 'I' to begin a conversation—I'm not good enough. I'm not smart enough,' just like the sketch from *Saturday Night Live*. And the worst: 'I hate myself.'

"That is not you. That is not me.

"Think back to the times in the silent retreats when you were meditating and you only felt love, when you tried to forgive the Taliban for killing your friend and you couldn't. Think back at how—even though you couldn't forgive them—you wished them no harm.

"That is you. That is me.

"You see beauty. You see light. You know that in the deepest part of your being, somehow, you are on the right path.

"You see it in a butterfly. You see it in the clouds. It

rains on you after a drought. You know it, as you know yourself, that the lesson is love.

"And you can fight it as hard as you like. You can deny your inner beauty for many more lifetimes. You can deny your connection to *me*. Each lesson will not change, and all must be learned."

As I listen, I gaze upon the countryside—the spirals of Cyprus trees reaching up into the sky, the day spilling out around them. A single strand of glimmering light—a lone hair—gliding on air, going nowhere, everywhere, nothing and everything. Such as it is with time.

"Your ego has a watch. But you, me, we exist together in the land of eternity."

Ode to MSF @ Kunduz

Clouded skies question the call to arms.
Late-breaking waves, building
Momentum for hours
Explode against the dropping sun.

As surfers scurry every which way,
The setting sun burns wildly
Within the hospital walls
On the other side of the world.

Breathless, the walls crumble.
Forty-two souls, as of today,
Rise from the ruins
And depart Kunduz.

The able-bodied wave off
The droning heart of the beast
As it clutches the air
Within their lungs.

Surgeons return to the matter
At hand, and the team,
Once again,
Works into the night.[3]

Bound by My Footsteps

*I*t was a week after the winter solstice, and the night was still falling heavily and too soon. Nearing the entrance, I passed by a woman who was curled around the edge of a wooden bench, her fingers clutching the splintered, rain-stained slats as she stared off into the distance. "She knows someone," I thought.

I moved slowly along a string of winter wreaths, lodged in unison atop the steel rods of the outer chain fencing. Potted domes planted into the earth cast the dim light of half-moons underfoot—their remains subsumed under the darkness below. The twins to these domes flickered faintly on polished granite slabs more than ten feet high. As the scores of moving bodies passed by them, the souls of 58,272 Americans were pulled along by a string of knowing eyes—one set with night vision, the other set seen only in dreams.

I passed a man clutching a camera as he steadied himself against the cold. Slowing, I tried to make out the string of dark shadows below. A handwritten love letter lay crumpled at the base of the wall among other mementos that also had been laid to rest in the darkness. The rumpled letter was somehow mysteriously lit. The other dark shapes wilted into the distance as I passed them.

I heard the snap of a camera shutter. Sweeping fresh

snowflakes from under his eyes, the man with the camera pushed off from the wall. After a few steps, he aimed again. I stopped and stood quietly. The man glanced up at me. In the darkness, I held his gaze until, methodically, he turned and tilted his head. I heard another snap.

The man let his camera drop hard against his chest. Thin light reflected off it as it hung lazily around his neck. Keeping my distance, I watched as the man slowly raised his right hand and placed it flat against the stone wall. Fending off the cold, I reached deeply into my silk-lined pockets, tightly grasping the warm softness within. Squaring my shoulders, I turned and walked on.

Though we were presumably from a different place and a different time, our experiences seemed eerily the same. This, no matter how deep the darkness, I clearly could read.

As the man neared the end of the walkway, so did I. His friends were awaiting him; he no longer was alone. Each touched his shoulder and whispered to him in the darkness. I veered off in the opposite direction and continued on my way.

Pulled by emotion, I stopped to look back. A throng of people moved steadily along the dim lights that cut into the night below. Bound by my footsteps, a long and steady string of lights trailed behind me. Twisting back into the night, I set out toward the boulevard, a long and steady string of lights afore.

Part Two

The Relativity of Choice

Surrender to Gaia

Inhale. We begin in child's pose, arms stretched out.
Heels back, hands square. Downward-facing dog.
I turn my head to track the passing breeze;
My eyes lock onto the rustling palm fronds.
Exhale. Return to all fours. Cat-cow. Five
At your own pace. In the pool, waves pop to
The surface in nickel-size swirls, twisting
As they reach back in time. Stand with your hands
To your heart. Breathe. Arms up, lean back. Micro-
Back bend. Fold forward. Cradle your elbows.
Lie down, head back, legs up. Fish pose. Release.
Surrender to Gaia. My arms and legs
Flop out. Savasana. As my heart takes
A bow, my mind flashes indigo blue.

Fun with Physics

The delivery truck arrived and backed
Into my yard at a ninety-degree
Angle. The logo painted on the side
Read: *Fun With Physics*. A cutout of a
Mini explosion was applied under
The word *Boom!* A single atom dotted
The exclamation. The beeping stopped, and
The driver jumped out of the cab. He climbed
Up onto the trailer, unlatched the door,
And it swung open. Inside lay millions
Of multicolored puzzle pieces. None
Were boxed. The driver pulled a large shovel
Off the trailer wall. Leaning on it, he
Asked, "Where would you like me to put these, ma'am?"

Radio Flyer

To the precipice, I drag my wagon.
It's been with me since childhood, and although
I have outgrown it, the wagon retains
Its heavy load. By now it's just a pile
Of mush, the weight of one human brain. Yet
The matter still tugs at me after all
These years. I ask God to take it from me.
"I no longer want to drag this behind
Me," I tell him. The wagon lights up as
Bright as an eight-point star. The handle drops
From my hand. Orion bends over and
Picks it up. The wheels roll into the sky—
In search of Pleiades, where the mother star
Of the Milky Way with warm cookies waits.

Falling to Grace

So many are my guilty pleasures—vice
Underscores this life of mine. My very
Reality, biting down the bones. Self-
Redemption scours the depths of "now."
Undereducated am I in the cloak of
Nondenominational consciousness.
Destiny unhinged. Purpose out of reach.
Current devoid of electricity.[4]
Refraction in opposition to *Source*.[5]
Time spinning pinwheels into a vacuum,
Oneness snaps open a ray of white light—
Godlike in its command of energy.
Opulence as fine as a well-aged wine,
Deepest desire the vibration of love.

The Sound of Silence

Under the green-gray haze, the sun is still.
A pelican slides by, its husky wings
Trailing a crusted beak. Dozens of boards
Paddle toward the impending horizon,
Beyond the swell. Lateral cliffs lay down
Upon the ocean floor, as holograms
Squirt out from the undersides of the small
Feet of children. As they stomp about, their
Laughter is released in half-notes stacked in
Thirds on the warm-cool breeze of winter. A
Full moon glides in on the rolling whitecap
Spray—an end-of-year lullaby. Sung by
The still, small voice within the breaking waves,
The sound of silence pours onto the beach.

If Midnight Were Noon

If midnight were noon, birds would sleep with eyes
Wide open. Crickets would feather their wings.
Strings of sunlight would form a translucent
Tube around the moon, consciousness would drape
Our souls in light—if midnight were noon...
I awake to the squawking of a wild
Flock of birds. I rise and peer through the blinds.
One half of the flock is fluttering, the
Other half rests upon the dewy leaves
Of a nearby tree. The hands of dawn pull
Back the night, awakening time. Faint rays
Of sunlight lull me back to sleep. As I
Shut my eyes, the birds coalesce, bond, and
Move on, their wings folding patterns of song.

Free Will to Choose

A Nobel Prize! Al-Khalili says, for
He who can explain for us the two-split
Experiment. Leave the crested waves. Let
Go the grains of sand. The magic lies not
In an explanation for the masses.
Science will advance itself. There is no
Need for such a lofty goal, if driven
By recognition. The true pioneer
Seeks wellness we can replicate with or
Without observation. We can shift our
Focus from outer perception to
Inner knowing, where healing gives form to
Health. We have free will to choose. What do *you*
Want to be, a particle or a wave?

Plasma Power

The plasma of stored memories, blood beats
Within an electromagnetic field
In space-time, free from dis-ease, until, in
One fell swoop, the whole of my body drops.
Malaria has brought me down. In a
Matter of days, my red blood cells have left
Me. More than eight pounds disappear into
Thin air. My consciousness reaches out in
Search of a higher octave. Beyond my
Physical and astral bodies, my soul
Plugs into a higher dimension[6] where
Vibrating membranes rebuild my blood. The
Memories of my heart are once again
Restored. With ease, on padded joints I stand.

Double-Blind Were We

(To Royal Raymond Rife and Wilhelm Reich)

Their battles waged beyond fear of science,
One might now say. The fear was that of man—
A rigid, unscientific sort. Rife
Once had made history, observing the
Center of a cancerous cell, nested
In a hierarchy of cells, each flush
With bacteria. Fractal in nature.
Spirals to infinity. Lost are the
Frequencies once believed to heal—a cloud
Of ashes on an ocean of orgone.
If the microscopes developed by Rife
Had all not been smashed to smithereens, we
Might be able to see differently.
One man's intuition rests on a field
Of possibilities—a lifetime of
Memories only he can resurrect.
Meticulous research with promising
Findings (what are the odds?) make not a quack.
Reich gave us bodywork. His breath work fueled
The flames of his passion, as his own work
Went up in smoke. Tons of it! Banned were his
Reich boxes—destroyed by the FDA.
Rife took to the bottle. Imprisoned, Reich

Died. A culture of ridicule consumed
These two men, simply because it was not
Their time. The search for lost remedies, which
When found, will warrant retrial. The study,
When it is designed, will be triple-blind.

The Great Halls of Science

As I stare at the pencil, eyes sharpened,
The pencil remains objectified. It
Does not float. Light does not dance a two-step
On either plane alongside that which my
Mind alone created. But if I gaze
In stillness with soft eyes, observation
Orchestrates the notes of each atom, in
Sync throughout space-time. This I do not grasp,
As once I had grasped the pencil. Sharp eyes
In consciousness gravitate back to lead.
If one mind transforms a pencil, what becomes
Of the "hard question" as collective
Minds gaze into the great halls of science?

The Shadow of Power

Animal or mineral are tallied
As material. The mass of planets
Plummets into the pale of measurement,
A mere statistic alongside height, weight,
The pressure of the air we breathe but may
Not hold. Mass is energy. Space is time
In a rotating world that only the
Mind of science dares define. One side of
A silver-headed coin, whose currency,
Calculated to the nearest penny,
Accounts for information as if it
Were supreme. "Yes," I say. "But what of all
The other sides? The subtle side? Does not
All exist in the shadow of power?"

Part Three

Both Sides of the Veil

The Cloak of Consciousness

As I drop my head, my awareness falls below my chin, and my breath carries me to where I need to be. A thread of silver light bends and refracts, repairing torn memories. As I sit in silence, a quilted cloak of consciousness unfolds.

Fight or Flight

Can you hear the birds as they flap their wings?
This is me as the color of sky. When
You are blue, in a *whoosh* I am gone. I
Didn't think you would miss me when you have
So many other bodies to keep you
Company. I prefer not to stay home;
It's so much easier to take flight. I
Have more fun with Casper, the friendly ghost.
With him, and the others, I play—stretching
My tether to the thinnest possible
Strand of light before I snap and jolt
You back into the present. Then I go
Back out again. But make me a home filled
With peace, and in a heartbeat I will stay.

White Light

I picked up the rose quartz and held it close
To my heart. "White light, white light, white light," I
Said aloud. Then I draped myself in an
Additional layer of green, healing
Light. Some say if you protect yourself with
Light, you acknowledge that dark energies
Exist. Better safe than sorry, I think
As I grab my keys. I start the engine
And back out of the drive. Once on the road,
"White light, white light, white light," I say aloud,
"That all I pass be filled with light, and that
Which lies ahead." I thank the archangels
But keep my hands tight on the wheel at ten
And two, in case I drive under a cloud.

Bach Flower Power

I dig in around the roots of the white
Rose bush, clearing away dead, fallen leaves.
I offer them to the wind. Dark blotches
On yellowed wings flitter in spirals as
They make their way downward. The next day the
Nose of a dog nuzzles them back into
The earth. The roots of wellness forever
Imprinted on fields of energy, I,
Too, have savored flora's transmutation.
Two drops, three times a day, transported on
Ether the essence to heal. Returning
The favor, I add two drops of the Bach
Remedy to the watering can, tilt
It over the bush, and douse the petals.

The Current of the Streetcars

As night falls, the current of the streetcars
Dims. Behind the cart, the crew grunts out a
"Heave ho!" A rippling sneeze explodes from the
Horse ahead, and Domenico glides with
The house under the crossing. In this same
City, in another time, the corners
Have streetlights. Flashes of yellow thread the
Darkness around me. I cross with caution—
My batteries are flat. The moon shines down
On me as I walk up Quincy Street. I
Quickly shower, pull back the covers, and
Lay down my tired bones. As I close my
Eyes, the conductor sounds the bell. I jump
Aboard, my hand tightly gripping the rail.

The Veil of Forgiveness

In the final days of her life, my great-auntie Theresa lay breathing under the watchful eye of her mother. Clad in thick stockings, an apron, and a hairnet, Rosa stared tentatively into the camera. As she sat in her kitchen, resting her arm on the corner of the Formica table, "Bulla Sheeta!" no longer reverberated off the walls. The house on Quincy Street was gone. The photo hung on the wall over Auntie Theresa's bed in the health-care facility where she spent her final years. That same photo held vigil at Auntie Theresa's funeral.

After Auntie Theresa died, I sat at my desk, staring out the window of my high-rise apartment. The Foshay Tower—the tallest building in Minneapolis when I was a child—stood at attention. Glass facades of the newer generations of high-rise buildings surrounded it. Yet I was alone when I heard the collective voices of my Italian ancestors call out to me.

"Heal yourself, and you will also heal us," they said.

Startled, I thought about what I was being told. I had always believed that we come to this earth to learn specific life lessons, but I had never considered that we continue to learn and to heal on the other side of the veil.

Yet, the souls of my ancestors were still woven together like the delicate stitching of my Auntie Theresa's wedding gown. Their hearts boxed up in the same state as the wedding dress in its later years—the rose-colored lace disintegrated in parts, the mantilla no longer of this world. But if one were to sprinkle the dress with rose petals, the sweet fragrance of the flowers would surely complement the soft hue of the fabric, forgiving any inadequacies in the lace.

My great-grandmother Rosa, who died before I was born, had brought forward the souls of her daughters as part of the message. The mission of healing my ancestors were challenging me to undertake promised to be far-reaching. By forgiving any inadequacies in the delicate stitching of my mother's heart, my own heart would be mended. And through my forgiveness, a long string of hearts would also be healed.

As I gazed out the window, the sun reflected off the dome of the nearby basilica, filling the sky in a mosaic of light.

"I will; I promise," I said aloud.

"Ti amo, Pupa," my great-grandmother said.

The Writing on the Window

*A*s I looked out through the window, my eye caught the glimmer of a large smudge. I drew my face closer. Five translucent letters hung lazily on the glass in front of me.

"Sorry," it said.

From two of the letters, tears dropped down the pane. A tube of lip balm had been used to write the word.

I placed my finger on the letter "o" and pulled it downward on the window, extending the initial, greasy smudge. I pulled my finger up to my nose, but I could not make out a scent. Stepping back, I turned my head from side to side, moving my body in the direction of the light and then against it. A miniature globe shone in the center of the word.

Who, I wondered, can claim that they have hurt me?

The clouds, which had otherwise sheltered the late spring snow, parted. Sunlight filtered in through the window, creating a shadow at the base of the letters suspended in front of me. I pulled the plastic top off the cylinder of minted balm and lifted my writing hand up to the window.

"I am sorry, too," I wrote.

When Spirit Calls

The light turned red as I neared the corner.
I put on my turn signal and waited.
I felt a nudge and heard a thought: *Drive one*
More block. I ignored it. I was nearly
Home. The thought became more persistent: *Drive!*
As the light turned green, my car rolled forward,
The wheel now firmly in my hands.
I parked next to the side entrance,
Under the dome. But for the choir on the
Altar, the basilica was empty.
In her hand, the Virgin held a single
Lily. Votives flickered at her feet. As
I dropped down on my knees, the choir sang out:
"Lord, make me an instrument of your peace."

The Climb to Assisi

Along the winding mountain road, the dust of footsteps is turned up by pilgrims. Headlights cut through the clouds. A car slowly passes—crushing pebbles, the only discernible sound. As the light thins, the pilgrims trudge on. Above the crest, a metal cross glints gold. One strike of the clapper turns copper to tin, stretching the universe over billions of years as the red shift of distant stars paints the sky. As the pilgrims settle into their makeshift camp, alchemists scurry to roll up the earth's canvas around them, chipping off and re-purposing cracked flecks of paint throughout the night. When the pilgrims rise, each is given an artist's palette covered in liquid gold. Before them, a fresh canvas unfolds. On this day, their individual signatures dissolve into one, and the true artist of creation is revealed. As the last bit of light is rolled into night, the canvas reads: *On Behalf of the Greater Good.*

Future Perfect

"Meet me in the plasma. I'll wait for you
There." I take a deep breath, and George appears.
He came to me as a white butterfly
When I was in Africa. "Hi, George!" I'd
Say. He flutters by and tells me, "One day
There will be more parties. There will be so
Many!" My heart drops back to a time when
We were young. Before I left the US.
Before he was gone. It does no good to
Argue. He trumps me every time. "You have
More work to do than I did!" He laughs. That
Wonderful, warm, heartfelt laugh. "Oh, right," I
Say. Another party must be starting—
A butterfly dips by and disappears.

Spirit Animal

Soft and subtle the rattling shakes as
My mind drops under the world. Before me
A swirl of color gives way to a wide
Array of animals. A pack of wolves,
The wings of a hawk, the belly of a
Hippo. The silver tail of a red fox
As it darts about, chasing them away.
For it is he who is mine. He circles
The stones of a fire pit, creating a
Sacred space. I enter on the skin of
Deer moccasins. The beating of the drums pulls
My feet into the claylike earth in a
Ceremonial dance. I am the fox,
We are the fire, rising in flames of smoke.

The Echo of a Whisper

Within the Seth Material, as channeled by Jane Roberts (1929–1984), I was asked to sense the source of power within my breath in order to connect to the life force within.

I put down the book, closed my eyes, and let the pencil I was holding slip out from between my fingers. I uncrossed my legs. I took a breath and followed it through my nostrils, down into my trachea. But it did not, surprisingly, lead me to inflated lungs. It did not, as it does on most days when I travel with it, settle into my heart.

This lone breath combined with a greater life force leading to a *coordinate point* at the center of my throat. For many years, at this very point in my physical body, I had experienced a periodic dull pain. I often felt a choking sensation. But until my consciousness followed my breath to this point in my body, I had not considered that the purpose of the pain was heralding me to more closely attend to the subtle aspects of my body in need of healing.

I listened more closely to my body as it hummed the melody of many lifetimes. Working with my physical and subtle bodies in meditation, I aligned them. I began integrating my physical, astral (emotional), and causal (soul) bodies on a daily basis. As they began to resonate as one, the dis-ease dissolved, and its imprint was carried away on the echo of a whisper.

Ask and It Is Given

Archangel Michael, please tell me what I need to do to release my fear so that I may be fully on the path to my higher life purpose.

"There is a part of you that is like Jell-O. And yet, you feel the weight of your worries. The past days have brought sadness. You no longer want to continue doing what you are doing in the home that is your skin. You want to spring free. And you know that there are many new things awaiting you. You want to be careful not to leave in a huff. But over the past few days, you have relied too heavily on your ego. Release the need to be right or good or celebrated. Instead, look for the truth, the goodness, and that which can be celebrated in others.

"Breathe in peace and breathe out the sadness. It is that easy. Breathe in peace and breathe out the sadness. There, I have said it again. Reflect on this for a moment...

"Breathe in and smile. Feel my loving presence on your shoulder. In your heart. Know that I am with you. With the infinite love I bring to you, how can life be dense? In the reflection of all that is, density is but an illusion.

"Breathe in the atmosphere of the new day each morning. Feel the wonderful lightness that is life. Your breath gives you wings—this is love. Take flight."

White Moon in a Powder Blue Sky

The days were short, but the sun was bright. A brisk wind cut into me as I neared the intersection. A white moon, nearly half-full, floated on a powder blue sky. As I waited for the cars to pass, a smug happiness poured over me. How wonderful to work a half day. I gathered the collar of my coat, pulling it tight to my chest. A flashing white light signaled me to cross. I grabbed onto my hat. The soles of my boots left the curb, and a gust of wind carried me away.

POSTSCRIPT

One morning, as I entered the kitchen of my apartment in Minneapolis, I noticed that one of the books lined up on the top of my fridge was askew. The books were firmly encased in a rack with wooden bookends. The rack held a dozen books, and they were always neatly aligned. I pulled the book that was askew out from the rack. It was a book on wine. I looked around the kitchen. On my counter, I had lined up three bottles of wine. It was the Christmas holiday week, and I had bought a number of bottles to bring with me to upcoming parties as hostess gifts. Like the books in the book rack, the three bottles had been neatly arranged on the counter the night before. Yet, this morning, one of the wine bottles was out of place. I picked up the bottle, looking for more clues. On the bottom of the label was a reference to Barone's Vineyard. Smiling, I looked up and said, "Hi, Grandma!" Barone's was my grandmother's favorite Italian restaurant in Van Nuys, California, close to where she had lived.

My grandmother Jeanette was stylish. Well into her eighties, she dressed and put on makeup each morning. Lancôme mascara accentuated the natural sparkle in her eyes when she laughed or made jokes. Twice after she had died, my grandmother came to me in spirit at the Lancôme makeup counter.

The first time this happened, I was shopping at a mall in Minneapolis with my sister, Susan. We split up, and I ventured over to the mascara display. There was a stack of flyers, promoting a free makeup session, next to the cabinet of mascara. The top flyer was signed. It read: *Julie*. I called my sister over and showed her the signed flyer on the top of the stack. We both marveled at how similar the writing was to her own.

A few years later, I was shopping by myself at another mall. Again, I went to the Lancôme counter, and to my surprise, there was also a stack of flyers next to the mascara display. The date of the event noted on the flyer was February 14. And once again, the top flyer was signed. It read: *Julie*. As I had done years earlier, I picked up the flyer, folded it, and put it in my purse.

Susan has kept the first flyer, with the writing similar to her own, and I have kept the second flyer, which I placed in the box that holds the gold charm bracelet bequeathed to me after my grandmother's death.

Susan had once asked me how she could also receive messages from our grandmother's spirit. I told her that all she needed to do was to look for the signs. In writing this, I realize that the first flyer was not meant for me at all but for her, since the handwriting on the flyer was similar to her own. At the time, I missed this clue. Perhaps this was why, years later, when shopping alone, I came across a second flyer under the Lancôme mascara case with my name signed on it. This was clearly a greeting for me.

For what purpose were these messages sent to my sister and me? To tell us hello and that there is still love among us. To receive messages of one's own, one simply needs to remain open for signs. When spirit or loved ones are attempting to deliver messages to us in the physical world, they use signs that we will recognize.

Doreen Virtue, PhD, who works with the angelic realm, has said that angels visit us through butterflies, feathers, and coins. This is the same with other spirits, including the spirits of our loved ones. They come through on the scent of their favorite flower or perfume, on smoke, or through the repetition of numbers or number sequences. They ride upon the resonance of music or words. They manipulate electricity and electronics or travel on flashes of light, for they are energy.

One need not be psychic to receive messages. We each can easily interact with vibration. Anyone can sit down at a piano and strike a middle C. But only with study and practice can we strengthen our skill in the making of music. Intuition is like music. It interacts with the field beyond our physical bodies where higher vibrations originate. To communicate with us in the physical world, spirit needs to lower its vibration. To receive messages from spirit, we need to heighten our awareness.

As it concerns our loved ones, we each know best the likes and dislikes, characteristics, senses of humor, and other idiosyncrasies of their personalities. Once deceased, they continue to exhibit these aspects when communicating with us. As in life, some of our loved ones communicate more openly or more clearly than others. It is the same when our loved ones cross over.

In addition to greetings, messages are also offered to promote soul-based healing and other learning for our higher good. As we listen to the wide range of frequencies within the many fields around us, both our loved ones and spirit alike fill these airwaves with messages. It is not always possible, however, to receive the exact message that we may desire to hear. But when we tune in for our higher good, no matter the content, the messages we receive will always arrive on the vibration of love.

AUTHOR'S NOTE

The study of subtle energy and the multidimensional body often results in an expanded awareness of self from both an inner and outer perspective. The inner journey allows for the personality of the current lifetime to align with the soul's contract, or chart of life lessons, outlined before incarnating. The journey into expanded consciousness often results in an increased awareness of the oneness of all things. The idea that there is a collective consciousness and our individual souls both spring from and feed into this all-encompassing energy becomes more apparent the deeper one looks inside oneself. We are timeless, our souls eternal. But when we cross over, we do not rest on our laurels. We continue to learn, grow, and contribute to the greater consciousness.

In the meantime, we are here on Earth. And no matter our greater purpose, we are still faced, in a time-bound shell, with the reality of our day-to-day lives and all of their joys, sorrows, challenges, and triumphs. In communities or in isolation, so many of us want to break out of our negative cycles, or molds. So we embark on a personal path of growth that we hope will be transformational. If we take this path, carried on the shoulders of our egos, we yearn for success and to be revered as phenomenal. But if we keep our focus on our higher selves and work each day in service of the greater good, we are instead presented with insights into the wonders of the phenomenon of the spirit world. This I have learned firsthand.

The more I studied, the more I became aware of my higher self. My heart opened. But I also felt an immense sense of responsibility. During an online course on intuition with the James Van Praagh School of Mystical Arts, I became overwhelmed. During office hours for the course, I joined the queue of students waiting in line to ask James questions about the content of the weekly lesson. When my call was selected, I shared my feeling of being overwhelmed with the heightened awareness of my intuitive gifts, not knowing what I should do with them.

In response, James told the class that through the study of our intuitive gifts (and we all have them), we gain a deeper understanding of the power that our intuition holds for us. By listening to our inner being, we were told, we could live our daily lives more confidently from a place of knowing. This was the same lesson put forward by Echo Bodine, although she referred to intuition as the still, small voice within.

With James's words in mind, I went into meditation. I was prepared to face my overwhelming fears and buckle up to any mission in life that I was destined to be given. I closed my eyes, and before me was darkness. In the center of it all was a catwalk, and at the end of the catwalk, a kneeler bathed in light. I stepped onto the catwalk and slowly approached the kneeler. I knelt down under the ray of light.

Looking up into the darkness beyond, I said, "OK, God, Source, All That Is, I am ready for my assignment." I held my breath, awaiting whatever workload was to be requested of me on my way forward. As I sat before them in meditation, they said to me, "Julie, we want you to live a happy life."

I released my breath, surprised at the simplicity of the mission. I had been ready and willing to undertake anything that would have been asked of me. But what I was being told, in essence, is that *life doesn't have to be so hard*—a lesson I am still struggling to incorporate into my life each day.

I share this personal experience with you, since even though it seems a simple task, it is perhaps one that is quite profound. What of beauty, light, and playfulness? The things of purity that we admire in children and that we wish for ourselves if there is a heaven? Does it not make sense to strive for these things in the here and now? For if we cannot see beauty, live through light, and delight in playfulness in our current lives, when, I wondered, do we learn these lessons?

From beyond the veil, my great-grandmother challenged me to undertake a lesson of self-healing. If successful, I was told, my own healing would not only positively affect her, it also would affect many others on both sides of the veil. As a result of this message, I now believe that we are not "anointed" with goodness and grace for eternity after we die. Goodness and grace must instead be learned throughout our many lifetimes.

The possibilities for self-directed, soul-based healing are infinite. The signposts along the way are many, and each points to a potential life lesson. And these lessons, which are personal in nature, need to be experienced as such. Each of us sees the pathways before us differently, and I encourage everyone to look inside of themselves to consider what their own, personal life lessons may be. In my life, judging by the many signposts that have stopped me in my tracks, I still have quite a bit of work to do. Some of my life lessons include patience, willpower, letting go of the need to control, the art of joy, and of course, love.

Impatience, frustration, and sadness exist within us all. These emotions, along with more positive ones, such as happiness, hopefulness, and excitement, provide us with important information as we live our lives each day. But to successfully live happy lives, we need only to get out more and play—a challenge sure to bring great benefit to each of us, should we choose to join in on the fun.

NOTES

1 According to Einstein's Theory of Relativity, we live in a four-dimensional reality: three spatial dimensions and one temporal dimension (the space-time). String Theory postulates the existence of many more, and, of course, spiritually oriented people also believe in many more dimensions of existence, where spiritual realms unfold.

2 From Hugo, Victor. *Les Misérables*. Translated by Norman Denny. New York: Penguin, 1982.

3 Médicins Sans Frontières (MSF), "Doctors without Borders" in English, is a global humanitarian relief organization. For years, I worked alongside this organization in many conflict zones. And even though I never worked directly for them, they were always my favorite humanitarian organization: *they got in, they got out, they saved lives*. In October 2015, the Trauma Treatment Center in Kunduz, Afghanistan, a hospital operated by MSF, was bombed by a US Air Force C-130. This piece is dedicated to the global MSF team, who have resumed their work providing medical services in Kunduz.

4 Electrical current is made up of electrical charges (electrons). Hence, electrical current is made up of electricity. Current is electricity in motion.

5 Refraction is an optical phenomenon in which a ray of light is deflected when passing through a medium; in this piece, by *Source*, the author is referring to the highest level of collective consciousness or "oneness."

6 As noted earlier, our physical reality is made up of four dimensions (three spatial and one temporal). There are other, higher dimensions we can access; these are not the common four dimensions that our physical senses perceive. They lie beyond our physical reach. Our subtle bodies easily access these higher dimensions, however.

ABOUT THE AUTHOR

*J*ulie R. Dargis is a poet, writer, and intuitive. Her healing practice includes oracle card readings, energy healing, and creative writing prompts to aid clients in achieving self-directed, soul-based healing. She is currently pursuing a PhD in integral health at the California Institute for Human Science, a research facility dedicated to the mind-body-spirit connection.

For more information, visit: www.juliedargis.com.

To share your own story of personal transformation and healing submit your writing in poetry or prose to: www.whitemooninapowderbluesky.wordpress.com.

If you need a writing prompt, center yourself with your breath, ask yourself a question to connect more closely with your higher self, and pull a card from the White Moon in a Powder Blue Sky Oracle Cards *deck. Use your intuition to find the resonance within the message, and then simply write from your heart.*

Made in the USA
San Bernardino, CA
28 July 2016